humanism
and libraries

Humanism and Libraries

An Essay on the Philosophy of Librarianship

By André Cossette

Translated and edited by Rory Litwin

Library Juice Press
Duluth, Minnesota

Copyright André Cossette, 1976

Translation and additional materials copyright Rory Litwin, 2009

Published in 2009

Published by Library Juice Press
P.O. Box 3320
Duluth, MN 55803
http://libraryjuicepress.com/

This book is printed on acid-free paper that meets present ANSI standards for archival preservation.

Cossette, André.
 [Humanisme et bibliothèques. English]
 Humanism and libraries : an essay on the philosophy of librarianship / by Andre Cossette ; translated and edited by Rory Litwin.
     p. cm.
 Includes bibliographical references and index.
 ISBN 978-1-936117-17-8 (acid-free paper)
 1. Library science--Philosophy. 2. Libraries--Aims and objectives. I. Title.
 Z665.C75813 2009
 020.1--dc22
                              2009039410

Contents

Preface	vii
Notes on the Translation	xiii
Publisher's Acknowledgements	xvii
Acknowledgements	xix
Introduction	1
Part 1: Concepts and Problems in the Philosophy of Librarianship	3
Chapter 1: What is Meant by "The Philosophy of Librarianship"	5
Chapter 2: The Lack of a Coherent Philosophy of Librarianship	17
Part 2: Elements of the Philosophy of Librarianship	29
Chapter 3: Definition of Librarianship	31
Chapter 4: The Ultimate Aims of Libraries	41
Conclusion	59
Questions for Reflection	63
References	65
Index	75

Preface

André Cossette, a librarian in Quebec, Canada, wrote the text presented here as an investigation of the foundations of the library profession. As you will see in his acknowledgments, it was written as part of a graduate program in Library Science at the University of Montreal. It was published in book form in 1976 by ASTED (L'Association pour l'avancement des sciences et des techniques de la documentation, more or less Quebec's version of the Special Libraries Association), under the title, *Humanisme et bibliothèques: Essay sur la philosophie de la bibliothéconomie.* Mr. Cossette, I very much regret to say, is no longer alive to accept my praise for his essay and to respond to questions and comments.

This text may strike many readers as an oddity during the present Library 2.0 era, when our discourse is so preoccupied with issues that had not yet been imagined at the time of its original publication. It was written in a very different context, and it asks basic, philosophical questions about the profession that don't occur to most American librarians to ask. Therefore, I feel that it rests on me to explain why librarians today ought to read Cossette's little book on library philosophy.

Unlike many of the books published by this press, the overall statement that Cossette's book makes is not radical (except insofar as it insists on the need for a carefully thought out philosophical underpinning for professional practice). Most of what it says would be met with agreement by mainstream American librarians who cut their teeth in library school and libraries at the time of its writing or in the decades that followed. However, if I am not mistaken, many readers may recognize in it ideas that are present within their own practice but which they have not before seen expressed in a systematic way. Cossette's intention was to build a foundation for the practice of librarianship that was a simple, solid and comprehensive structure, and not a mixture of diverse ideas that sound appealing but are never thought through one against another. This is not a familiar approach for American librarians. We tend to find our philosophical foundations, such as they are, in inspiring statements of ideals that become fuzzy when inspected closely or juxtaposed, but find them useful enough to keep us going. We are generally not concerned with their logical connections or lack of connections.

Cossette's essay begins with the complaint that modern librarianship lacks a clear philosophy. I would speculate, over what I imagine would be some objections, that it took a librarian from the Francophone world to be piqued enough by this observation to set about finally working out the foundations for the profession in philosophical terms at a time when the practice of librarianship had already reached such a mature phase. I think that this is the case for two reasons. First, it is because modern librarianship, with its emphasis on intellectual freedom and support for democracy, has been very much an Anglo-American cultural development. It was a combination of both the neighboring Anglo-American tradition and the more elitist French tradition that shaped the library context of Quebec. This means that in Quebec in the mid 70s there would have been somewhat more of a reason to work out and state in clear terms what may have been more internalized and intuitively accepted, if not fully thought through, south of the border. Secondly (and this may be utter BS, but seems true to me), Francophone culture is relatively more interested in and receptive to philosophical discussion than American culture, which tends to prefer a practical approach. (Cossette himself identified the more practical and less theoretical orientation of Anglo-American culture as one of the reasons that a true philosophy of librarianship had not yet been worked out.) If Cossette's book is typically Francophone in approaching librarianship from a seriously philosophical perspective, however, one should not assume that its philosophy is "typically French," and reminiscent of French developments in late 20th century philosophy and literary theory. Cossette drew upon a philosophical tradition that I think Anglo-American readers will be comfortable with, and liked his statements clear, simple and definite.

Readers may be asking a couple of questions at this point. The first question I can image being asked is, Why should American librarians be interested in a philosophical treatment of the foundations of the profession if it simply states in a systematic fashion what we already intuitively understand and picked up in a different way in library school and in the professional literature? The answer is that Cossette's work, in fact, does not only state systematically what we already understand; reading it tells us other things as well. In working through the ideas that underlie the profession in a systematic way, we become aware of the internal logic of what we do, which can be a great source of confidence in the decisions that we make. At the same time, we also become aware of the internal contradictions in much of what we have not really examined about our own practice, and may become aware of some new facets of our professional foundations, with consequences for our approach to our work. Furthermore, in addition to this logical working-out of what otherwise goes unexamined, Cossette gives us a useful historical perspective on the intellectual foundations of the profession. Sound ideas about what librarianship is and what its goals are permit us to claim a degree of autonomy in institutions where we might otherwise serve as mere functionaries rather than as the professionals we are. Without a philosophical foundation, we lack a basis for making decisions regarding how to change our institutions in response to external forces, with the potential result that we do not play the role that we should in decision-making.

The other question that I can imagine being asked by readers at this point is, What is the relevance of a library philosophy of 1976, however solid, to the questions faced by librarians in an era when everything has changed and continues to change rapidly? The answer I would give is that philosophy, of all of the disciplines that can be applied to a study of the profession, is the only one that has a sufficient degree of abstraction and generality to remain valid and instructive over a period of time during which so many of the methods and even contexts of use have been overturned. A philosophy of librarianship is more serviceable than a science of librarianship (see Cossette's distinction in the first chapter) in providing a source of continuity regarding what librarianship is and what it is for. That continuity, and clear sense of identity and purpose that come from it, are necessary to guide us through a sea of change (to use a corny metaphor) without running aground, going adrift, or being smashed to bits by the results of decisions that fail to take our destination and the big picture into account. The future of librarianship is not guaranteed. To those who do not view librarianship as being a distinct and self-defined profession carrying some kernel of continuity with its history based on a conceptual identity, that isn't of much importance. Understanding librarianship through a philosophy of its foundations rather than through its contingencies makes it matter, and highlights the importance of its continuation. I hope contemporary readers will find the book useful in this regard.

Rory Litwin
Duluth, MN
October 4th, 2009

Notes on the Translation

There are a number of key terms and groups of terms in Cossette's text that do not map well onto an English vocabulary and are therefore difficult to translate. I should explain how I resolved some of these difficulties.

A primary problem is in the term *bibliothéconomie*, which means librarianship or library science. The parallel to our older term "library economy" is evident. In most cases I translated the term as "librarianship," so that I could translate his phrase "*science de la bibliothéconomie*" as "science of librarianship" or sometimes "library science." The basic reason this issue is confusing has more to do with the oddity of the English term "library science," indicating a body of knowledge that is part art and part science. I have tried to use "librarianship" to refer to the practice of the profession, including the knowledge that a professional requires to do the job; "library science" or "science of librarianship" to refer to the academic, scientific discipline that creates new knowledge for the profession; and "philosophy of librarianship" or sometimes "library philosophy" to refer to a philosophical investigation of the underpinnings of professional practice. There were cases when this formulation was not easy to apply, so I want readers to be aware of it.

Many French words translate directly to English and are spelled nearly the same. The exceptions tend to be the words that can illustrate how a language carries with it a way of thinking. Two French words that make me love the language are the verb *faire* (and its noun form *un fait*) and the noun *un projet*.

Faire is a very basic and common verb meaning both "to do" and "to make." The noun *un fait* means a doing or a making, that is, something done or made, which also means a fact, or an accomplishment. Cossette often writes of *les faits* of libraries, meaning the facts of libraries, but with an implication rooted in the language that those facts are the result of what has been done in libraries, what librarians have created. The word for "fact" then, or at least that word for a fact, reminds us to take nothing as a given, and its broader usage covers a number of other English words. A fact that is to be considered as a given, that is, as data, is called *une donnée*, from the verb *donner*, which means to give. Cossette used both words frequently in the text. I translated these words differently according to the context and my sense of his meaning, using the words, "activities," "acts," "facts," "events," "realities," "happenings," "doings," "observations," "actualities," or "data."

The noun *projet* partially maps onto our noun "project," and is likewise related to a verb form (*projeter*), and comes from the same root. In French the meaning of the noun is closer than the meaning of the verb than it is for us: it means a plan, a practical projection-forward of an idea. Depending on the context, I translated the word variously as "project," "plan," "perspective," or "projection forward."

Two words that Cossette uses frequently and sometimes in the same sense are *une specialiste* and *un theoriste*. (The latter is an unusual alternative to the word *theoricien*.) Their literal meanings are similar to their evident English equivalents, but in the context of the book it was not so simple to use the equivalent English words. According to the meaning in context, I translated these words as "professors," "thinkers," "writers," "researchers," "theorists" and "specialists."

Finally, the word that gave me the most trouble in attempting to make Cossette's ideas comprehensible in English was the French word *la science*, which means science, but in a broader sense. Less than 100 years ago, our word "science" also communicated a broader meaning, denoting an intellectual approach to a subject that is systematic and empirical, in contrast to the more intuitive and traditional approach of "the Arts." In French the word *science* continues to convey this broader meaning, rather than the more narrow reference to academic disciplines that use the "scientific method," especially where that method is strictly regulated. This difference in meaning presented a challenge in conveying Cossette's intentions in Chapter 3, where he discussed the epistemology of librarianship. I used the words "science" and "scientific," but also "evidence-based," "rationality," and "systematic," according to the context.

Rory Litwin
Duluth, MN
October 4th, 2009

Publisher's Acknowledgements

As mentioned in the Preface, this book was originally published in 1976 as *Humanisme et bibliothèques: Essay sur la philosophie de la bibliothéconomie*, by ASTED (L'Association pour l'avancement des sciences et des techniques de la documentation).

Francis Farley-Chevrier, Director of ASTED, and Marcel Lajeunesse, a professor at the library school at the University of Montreal, were generous with their time in helping me resolve questions regarding the copyright status of Cossette's work. I would like to thank them for their cooperation.

I would like to thank the University of Minnesota, Duluth, for granting me a leave for working on the translation of Cossette's book. I am indebted to my institution for this support.

I would also like to give a special thanks to Larry Oberg. Larry gave me encouragement, helped me with some rough spots in the translation, and reassured me that this first time translation effort was on track.

Rory Litwin
Duluth, MN
October 4, 2009

Acknowledgements

Thanks are due to professors Marcel Lajeunesse, Yves Courrier and Jean-Pierre Chalifoux of the the Library School at the University of Montréal, as well as our colleagues at the Collège de Trois Rivières: Claude Brouillette of the Department of Languages, Yvon Paillé of the Department of Philosophy and Jean-Louis Longtin, Deputy to the Director of Educational Services, who agreed to read this manuscript and gave judicious comments.

Special recognition is due to Ms. Janina-Klara Szpakowska, professor at the Library School at the University of Montréal, who agreed to direct this project in the context of an Independent Study. Without constantly relying on my research director, who benefited the project with her ideas, her criticisms, and her suggestions for important restructuring, this study would, without a doubt, never have been realized.

—André Cossette

Introduction

Contemporary librarianship is characterized by a fight for the full development of its theoretical foundations. This struggle against the claims of everyday practice and the empiricism of "Library Science" is fought on two fronts. The first is made of a clear and distinct desire to constitute librarianship as a scientific discipline. It aims to apply the scientific method to the library field as a way of providing methods that are understandable and effective. This concern for scientific rigor is largely accepted in the profession today and is on the road to progressively greater realization.

The second front has been pursued by a handful of solitary thinkers who have an awareness of the insufficiency of the scientific approach, and have their beginnings in the founding, in 1926, of the Graduate Library School of the University of Chicago. After 1930, the instructors at this celebrated library school would go on to work out, over roughly the next decade, the basic ideas of a philosophy of librarianship. Faced with indifference, the further development of a philosophy for the profession went forward principally because of the work of J. Periam Danton, Jesse Shera and D. J. Foskett, who established that while librarianship as a human activity had become a science, in reaching this status it need not bypass the essential questions in terms of which it must justify itself, its reason for being. These individuals' interest in the philosophy of librarianship demonstrates a remarkable lucidity and a clear will to go past the traditional pragmatism of the profession.

It is important, to be sure, to work for the improvement of the techniques used in libraries, but it is also important to take an interest in the ends that we want to achieve by them. It is necessary to provide the rational foundations for the beliefs that the librarians have in the value of their work. Noticing that the professional literature leaves questions of philosophy to the side in order to limit itself to questions of technique, the library theorists who have been the most conscious of this made the development of the fundamental concepts of the discipline their priority. These concepts are essential to safeguard the unity of librarianship and to avoid its fragmentation into multiple independent activities.

I am stating emphatically that librarianship has been pointed in a resolutely scientific direction. This orientation, sufficiently well established to mark a point of no-return, no longer permits us to identify the discipline as an agglomeration of techniques without any coherence. It is necessary to clarify, at the same time, that the conceptual scheme of librarianship is still relatively undeveloped. This theoretical weakness has given birth to the misunderstandings and misinterpretations of the relevance and meaning of the philosophy of librarianship that this essay endeavors to clear up. This philosophy, itself not well developed, has been described by specialists as unsystematic. Here, I attempt to determine the causes and analyze the consequences of this situation for the development of the profession.

This study has as its essential object to analyze the fundamental concepts elaborated by the firsts theorists of library philosophy as a way of separating the nature of librarianship from its technical practices and defining its ultimate aims. The central thesis is that the fundamental problem of the discipline is not one of technique but of ends. What goals guide the library in bringing about the full flowering of humanity? The ultimate intention here is to underline the profoundly humanistic character of librarianship.

Part 1

Concepts and Problems in the Philosophy of Librarianship

Chapter 1
What is Meant by "The Philosophy of Librarianship"

Terminological Issues

The philosophy of librarianship is essentially the posing of a radical question concerning the activities of the profession. It doesn't ask how to organize libraries, but goes to the root of things in asking the fundamental question: why libraries?

The answer to this question is equivalent to the determination of the ends, or goals, of libraries. The philosophy of librarianship consists, then, of research into the ends that justify the existence of libraries. It inquires into the ultimate purpose of librarianship. While its basic problem is the determination of ends rather than means, it does not leave the consideration of methods and techniques completely to the side. It has the function of evaluating whether those methods, or means, genuinely contribute to the attainment of the ends pursued.[1]

The philosophy of librarianship is that theoretical foundation for the discipline that is concerned with constructing a systematic "core" of general concepts necessary for the unification of the multiple ideas and practices belonging to the world of libraries.[2] It can be thought of as an endeavor of reflective research into the profound meaning that underlies "Library Science."

---

[1] Redmond A. Burke, "Philosophy of librarianship," *Catholic Library World*, 19 (October 1947), 13.
[2] J. Periam Danton, "Plea for a philosophy of librarianship," *Library Quarterly*, 4 (October 1934), 528.

Philosophy and Science

To better grasp the notion of the philosophy of a discipline, like the philosophy of librarianship, compare it to the idea of a science. A science is fundamentally the accumulation of observations; their interpretation or their description for the purpose of definition, analysis and classification; their explanation through research into their causes, and, finally, the testing of these explanations and the formulation of laws.[3] Science is characterized by a positive study of phenomena. The philosophy of a discipline, on the other hand, is concerned with the principles at the root of that discipline: its aims, its objectives and its broader function.[4] Science wants to know "How," while philosophy aims at the "Why." Thus, the educational sciences study the means of education, while the philosophy of education is concerned with the question: Why should you be educated?

Science	*Philosophy*
Positive study of phenomena	Study of basis and purpose
Research into the "how"	Research into "why"
Concerned with facts or events	Concerned with values
Experimental method	Reflective method
Treats people as objects	Affirms that people, as subjects, are the source of meaning

---

[3] A. K. Mukherjee, *Librarianship, Its History and Philosophy*, London, Asia Publishing House, 1966, p. 6.
[4] *Ibid.*, 6.

Science and philosophy both seek to construct theories to explain reality. It is important, however, to avoid thinking of scientific theory and philosophical theory as the same kinds of things; their difference consists essentially in the methods employed: one results from the application of experimental method, while the other develops out of a method of reflective thought. A scientific theory is a systematic collection of propositions that aims to explain the phenomena of some field delimited from reality as a whole; that is to say to determine the constituent relationships among the phenomena of that field, in a word, to discover their structure. The goal of all science consists simply in the elaboration of a theory, an ever-more comprehensive conceptual model that unifies and explains the facts of a sector of reality.

As for philosophical theories, one may define them as a systematic discourse on the basis or the purpose of a reality or of a subject. If that subject is defined as a particular discipline, that philosophical discourse has as its aim, then, to extract that discipline's essential principles. This unusual sort of discourse is so rarely seen that a specialist in technical methods and their studies might easily place it within the domain of his own scientific discourse. Indeed, H. Goldhor, emphasizing the criticisms set forth by J. Periam Danton and Jesse H. Shera regarding the absence of a philosophy of librarianship, asked whether these thinkers didn't feel the need for "more theories of substantive relationships,"[5] that is to say, scientific theories.

---

[5] Herbert Goldhor, *An Introduction to Scientific Research in Librarianship,* Urbana (Illinois) University of Illinois, Graduate School of Library Science, 1972, 71-72. (Monograph, no. 12).

To completely avoid confusion and better distinguish between the concepts of scientific discourse in librarianship, or library science, and philosophical discourse in the same discipline, or library philosophy, it seems necessary to better define each of these ideas.

The science of libraries, or "Library Science," is the theoretical construction of objective relationships among the activities of librarianship. If this approach, which aims to grasp the objective logic of the world of libraries, is viable, it is because there exist, in the activities of librarianship themselves, external relationships, necessary and not innate, that cannot be known by simple reflection, but only indirectly by observation and experimentation. This experimentation, or objective research, that is the condition of the possibility of a scientific practice of librarianship is not, for all that, reducible to an empiricist schema. The scientific method, in fact, does not rest on experimentation alone, on a simple reading of observations, but consists, in part, of an organization or structuring that arises out of the activities of the observer as such. One must be aware that pure empiricism is impossible in science, that the object of scientific study is knowingly and methodically constructed by a subject before experimental testing, and that observations are necessarily followed by a phase of interpretation which necessitates the involvement of a structuring of ideas that comes from the experimenter himself.

While library science is limited to objective knowledge of the activities within libraries, the philosophy of librarianship wants to account for the total experience of the profession, and includes questions of value. Contrasted to science, it necessarily consists of judgments of value that translate a vision of the world into the social engagement that follows from it. The philosophy of librarianship, then, is the theoretical integration of library practice as a unity, the encompassing understanding of the meaning of the profession. Through a method that is at once critical and reflective, it attempts to form a synthetic whole out of the disparate facts of librarianship to better direct its application.

The fundamental difference between library science and library philosophy resides in the fact that science is impersonal, makes an abstraction out of its subject, the person who lives in the world of libraries; while scientific theory places the individual person in a network of deterministic causes, philosophical theory does not consider the person as a thing among other things, but as a subject, a being in the world, who is engaged in it, and who by that fact gives it meaning. A philosophy of librarianship is called for because behind the phenomena of libraries one finds a subject, a person, a conscious and free being who is implicated in the world of the library, who is engaged in it in a particular way, and in that engagement arrives at his point of view on the world. It is important to state that the world of libraries would make no sense other than through the presence of a person, a subject, whose subjectivity brings forth a world seen through a point of view, and who gives meaning to things by the mediating function of his perspective. It is the person as subject who gives meaning and value to libraries by the purposes to which he puts them. The work of librarianship is a defining activity that gives a meaning, a comprehensive attitude toward humanity and the world. So, philosophical reflection applied to librarianship has for its goal precisely to make that meaning explicit. It attempts to give the world of libraries, which does not have a meaning in itself in terms of its objective description, a meaning and significance that results from deliberate judgment and the explicit statement of its purposes.

For a philosophy of librarianship, it is essential to reflect on the foundations and purposes of the profession, to question its nature, values, and limits, and to meditate on the final meaning of the project of librarianship. This research into "meaning," moreover, characterizes the philosophic enterprise generally.

The work of Ranganathan: Normative Principles or Scientific Principles?

Scholars in librarianship have not always recognized the distinction between science and philosophy. This lack of clear vision has, moreover, provoked, among many, a certain confusion concerning the theoretical basis of the discipline.

Vleeschauwer, for example, ignores the specificity of philosophy when he writes that "the word philosophy may perhaps sound more erudite and mysterious than theory or science, but it is nothing else than a pretentious synonym for these."[6] That expresses without a doubt his negative attitude regarding the possibility of a philosophy of librarianship.

The less-than-rigorous use of the term "philosophy" in the profession explains the less-than-pertinent interpretation that has been given up until now, to my mind, to that celebrated work of Ranganathan, *The Five Laws of Library Science*.[7] Numerous thinkers have seen in that work a philosophical study of librarianship. Chatterjee, notably, wrote: "Dr. S. R.

---

[6] H. J. Vleeschauwer, "Ambiguities in the present-day library," *Mousaion*, no. 36 (1960), 4.
[7] S. R. Ranganathan, *The Five Laws of Library Science,* Madras, 1957.

Ranganathan has condensed the whole philosophy of librarianship into five fundamental laws."[8] Foskett effused in the same sense: "the most sustained attempt to work out a philosophy of librarianship is that of Dr. Ranganathan."[9] In the same way, H. McMullen saw, in that work of Ranganathan, a discourse of sufficient complexity to merit the title of philosophy.[10] Finally, Mukherjee, evidently aware of the eccentric character of the work of the Indian librarian as a so-called study of library philosophy, qualified it as an "operational philosophy of librarianship."[11]

For my part, I do not hesitate to call this interpretation into question and to doubt the designation of Ranganathan's book as philosophy. Thinkers who have been interested in his work have poorly understood its profound meaning. Their position is likely due to the ambiguity of the work itself.

Ranganathan reveals, at the start of his book, his final intention: to reduce the numerous empirical facts of the world of libraries to a small number of basic principles.[12] His goal, simply put, is to apply the scientific method to librarianship, which he considers one of the social sciences. It is evident that the Indian librarian sought to make a scientific study of

---

[8] Amitahba Chatterjee, "Philosophy in librarianship," *Library World,* 7 (July-October 1964), 136.
[9] D. J Foskett, *The Creed of a Librarian – No Politics, No Religion, No Morals,* London, Library Association, 1962, p. 8 (Occasional paper, no. 3)
[10] Haynes McMullen, "Research in backgrounds in librarianship," *Library Trends,* 6 (October 1957), 111.
[11] A. K. Mukherjee, *Librarianship…,* 31.
[12] S. R. Ranganathan, *The Five Laws…,* 20.

librarianship more than to lay the basis for a philosophy of the discipline. Ranganathan thought, perhaps naively at that, that the formation of his five laws, which followed from the application of the scientific method, had provided a definitive foundation for librarianship as a science.[13]

But Ranganathan had a rather ambiguous conception of the social sciences. He confused the social sciences with the philosophy of the social sciences.

> In the social sciences, such as education, political science, economics, sociology, law, and library science – which is also one of them – the fundamental laws, are called normative principles."[14]

To affirm, as Ranganathan does, that the social sciences result in the formulation of normative principles would be to completely misunderstand the positive character of the social sciences. Its final ends are not at all to create normative principles, judgments of value, or a picture of the way things ought to be, but to state the existence of regular patterns and necessary relationships among social facts, that is, to examine society as it is. The social sciences, in a way that is like no other science, for that matter, are positive because they study what is, not what should be. The notion of a normative science is entirely contradictory. "Science does not make judgments of good and bad. It can not pass from what is to what ought to be."[15] No science can dictate rules of conduct, whether for the individual or the collective. A

---

[13] *Ibid.*, 368.
[14] *Ibid.*, 365.
[15] Maurice Duverger, *Méthodes des sciences socials*, 3rd ed., Paris, Presses Universitaires de France, 1964, p. 37.

field of study that seeks to establish what ought to be in human society is not a science but rather a social philosophy.

Based on the preceding reflections, we can conclude that *The Five Laws of Library Science* is a work of science expressed in a philosophical language. Ranganathan wants to uncover the laws of librarianship, which constitutes a scientific method, using a language that lets us believe it is philosophy. It is this ambiguity in the thought of Ranganathan that has led his followers to their incorrect interpretation. They believe that they have found a philosophy of librarianship because the author spoke of "normative principles," while it is very much a matter of science. Likewise Benge is fooled.[16] To my knowledge, only Richard Emery has had doubts about the validity of the traditional interpretation of Ranganathan, without going any deeper, when he wrote: "The fact that Ranganathan's laws are often referred to in terms of philosophical discussion is evidence of lack of clarity in theoretical discussions of librarianship."[17]

A Philosophy of Librarianship: Is It Possible?

Richard Emery answered this question with a categorical "No." He held that a philosophy of librarianship could not exist.[18] He further asserted the "banality of the phrase 'phi-

---

[16] Ronald C. Benge, *Libraries and Cultural Change,* London, Clive Bingley, 1970, p. 246.
[17] Richard Emery, "Philosophy, purpose and function in librarianship: The Library Association Prize Essay, 1971," *Library Association Record,* 73 (July 1971), 128.
[18] *Ibid.,* 128.

losophy' when applied to librarianship."[19] To justify these statements he stated that a philosophy of the profession is impossible because librarianship is a secondary occupation. And it is a secondary occupation because it neither creates nor applies its own knowledge.[20]

Before discussing Richard Emery's arguments, let me simply say that I do not find it more banal to discuss the philosophy of librarianship than to discuss the philosophy of economics or the philosophy of education. The qualification that this English thinker uses to designate a professional philosophy has the appearance of an unfounded assertion. He holds that librarians perform a secondary function because they create no new knowledge, but rather are occupied with the transmission of knowledge. Curious argument! To my knowledge, no professional, whether he is a doctor, a professor, or a psychologist, creates new knowledge in practicing his profession. One could add that neither does an instructor in professional education create that profession. There are researchers, applying the same standards to theory as to practice, who have produced and who advance each of these disciplines. A practicing psychologist, for example, does not create and has not created his discipline's knowledge base, but he has the application of the principles psychology, which he has learned. If one follows Richard Emery's logic to its conclusion, one has to affirm that that all professionals are working in secondary occupations. And that is absurd.

For Emery, librarianship can be qualified as a secondary activity for the reason that librarians do not apply their own

---

[19] *Ibid.*, 128.
[20] *Ibid.*, 128.

theoretical knowledge base. This argument supposes, more or less, a reduction of librarianship to pure technique. Is this reduction legitimate or does it come from an anachronistic conception?

The history of science permits us to note the historical and logical primacy of technique in the sciences. All of the sciences have been preceded by a phase of technical problem solving that produced questions, technology, and a method of control. Librarianship is not an exception to this rule. From the simple technique that defined the field until the middle of the 20th century, librarianship has progressed steadily until now, when it has approached the status of a scientific discipline with a role for methodology.[21] That is why it is imprecise to equate librarianship with a simple set of techniques, because many of the activities of librarians, to a significant extent, follow from an application of theoretical knowledge.

The work of librarians today very much resembles that of educators. Educators, transmitting knowledge that they have not produced pertaining to disciplines that they have not created, nevertheless apply a discipline of their own, that of education. It is the educators themselves, or more precisely the specialists who do fundamental research in education, who have created the science of pedagogy. Likewise, librarians, also communicating knowledge that they have not produced themselves, no less apply a particular theoretical knowledge base that has been created by researchers and specialists in library science.

Librarians have no reason to envy educators or other professionals regarding their professional roles. Their work is

---

[21] See Chapter III

no more secondary than that of any other specialist. To affirm the contrary and deduce that a philosophy of librarianship is impossible would be absurd. Just as the philosophy of education undeniably exists, it is evident that a philosophy of librarianship is in itself not at all an impossible enterprise. The profession at large, however, regardless of whether it's foundations are scientific or not, lacks the sense of a need for a philosophy of librarianship for understanding its aims: [22] "Any field or area of knowledge can have a philosophy. Indeed, without a philosophy a field of knowledge cannot be said to exist formally."[23] Librarians should stop being so unsure about the legitimacy of discussing a philosophy of librarianship. The expression has a real meaning and is valuable, regardless of Benge's judgment of it as not being particularly useful.[24] Thinkers in the field would not go wrong to define it as an investigation into the ultimate ends of librarianship.

Is this definition perhaps yet too limited? We have forgotten that a philosophy of a discipline equally includes an analytical aim: a critical study of its foundations. More than merely reflecting on ends, a complete philosophy of librarianship must rethink the concepts, categories, and theories forged by its specialists in order to determine their systemic value.

---

[22] A. K. Mukherjee, *Librarianship...*, 6.
[23] John M. Christ, *toward a Philosophy of Educational Librarianship*, Littleton, (Colo.), Libraries Unlimited, 1972, p. 14.
[24] Ronald C. Benge, *Libraries...*, 244.

Chapter 2
The Lack of a Coherent Philosophy of Librarianship

If theorists diverge regarding the relevance of "philosophy" applied to librarianship, there is one point on which they agree: that there is an absence of a coherent philosophy of the discipline.

Library science is still in a time of pragmatism. Librarians know how to do their work, but do not respond in a systematic way to the primordial question: why do this work?

> "We have pragmatic rules, like those found in a cook book, but of greater importance is the reason for these procedures. Past emphasis has been on activity and not on the value of the activity itself."[25]

J. Periam Danton expressed better than anyone the absence of a systematic philosophy of librarianship in an article that, although written decades ago, remains pertinent.

> "It requires little or no proof to state that the profession has never set forth a complete inclusive statement of its philosophy; that no such statement exists is well enough known ... There has certainly been no single, comprehensive philosophy of librarianship, and the isolated articles and addresses of a philosophical nature have been, in the first place too few, in the second place either too limited or too general, and, finally, totally incapable of being co-ordinated into a unified whole."[26]

---

[25] Redmond A. Burke, "Philosophy...," 12.
[26] J. Periam Danton, "Plea for a philosophy...," 529.

For librarians, the fact of not having a coherent professional philosophy does not prevent them from being motivated by ideas and principles, but these bear more resemblance to religion than to a genuine philosophy.[27] Those few tentative formulations of a professional philosophy, such as those of Jesse Shera, A. K. Mukherjee or A. Broadfield, point to but do not attain the profundity and development of the knowledge bases of other social sciences.[28] The theoretical foundations that determine the fundamental principles and concepts of librarianship have not yet been established in a coherent way. This lack is not limited to librarianship. Many other professions are deprived of a well-elaborated, special philosophy of their own.[29]

Causes

In investigating the causes of the lack of a coherent philosophy of librarianship, it is necessary to first look at the training traditionally given to librarians. In Europe, for example, it had generally been felt that on-the-job training is the best preparation for entrance into the profession, with periodic examinations to allow candidates to advance to higher levels. The profession was committed to the idea that practical training acquired through apprenticeships was the best training for the work of a librarian. Schools of library science were practically non-existent. *L'Ecole nationale superior de bibliothécaires* in Paris was not founded until 1963, and

---

[27] H. E. Bliss, "As to a philosophy for librarianship," *Library Quarterly*, 5 (April 1935), 234.
[28] John M. Christ, *Toward a philosophy...*, 15.
[29] H. E. Bliss, "As to a philosophy...," 233-234.

while the library school at the University of London was created in 1919, British library directors would not hire its graduates for many years, considering their training too theoretical.

In the United States, one of the most developed countries in the domain of library science, the training of librarians long resembled that of Europe, even if their system evolved more quickly. Apprenticeships in libraries were the only preparation possible prior to 1887. That year, Melvil Dewey founded the first school of librarianship, not only in the United States but in the world, at Columbia University in New York. The course of study was eminently practical, including only very little in the way of theory. Despite the formation of this school, many librarians continued to hold that apprenticeships were the best training. It is important to look at the publication of the celebrated report of C. C. Williamson in 1923,[30] because it definitively showed the deficiencies of the apprenticeship system and the need for real schools of librarianship within universities. It was not until the publication of this report that the profession realized that its theoretical basis was important, and librarians began to accept the relative importance of theory over practice in library education.[31]

As a result of the lack of theory in academic training and apprenticeships for in the profession, there is a near-total indifference toward theory among librarians. Pierce Butler,

---

[30] C. C. Williamson, *Training for Library Service: a Report Prepared for the Carnegie Corporation of New York*, New York, 1923.
[31] Josefa E. Sabor, *Méthodes d'enseignement de la bibliothéconomie*, Paris, Unesco, 1966, p. 86. (Manuels de l'Unesco á l'usage des bibliothèques).

in a work that has become a classic, made plain this shortcoming of traditional librarians:

> Unlike his colleagues in other fields of social activity the librarian is strangely uninterested in the theoretical aspects of his profession. He seems to possess a unique immunity to that curiosity which elsewhere drives modern man to attempt, somehow, an orientation of his particular labors with the main stream of human life. The librarian apparently stands alone in the simplicity of his pragmatism: a rationalization of each immediate technical process by itself seems to satisfy his intellectual interest. Indeed any endeavor to generalize these rationalizations into a professional philosophy appears to him, not merely futile, but positively dangerous."[32]

Butler had good reason to point out the conceptual weaknesses of the discipline, but he was a victim of these himself. Like most other theorists, he confused library science and library philosophy. His imprecision with these terms has already been remarked upon by the perceptive J. Periam Danton, who mentioned that Butler had not properly distinguished between these two concepts, and that he had used the terms almost as synonyms.[33]

What Butler criticized in librarians was their failure to elaborate scientific theories to explain the procedures used in libraries, and not, as he wrote, their not having produced "a professional philosophy." The American library theorist was correct to emphasize that librarians' exclusive interest in practical questions led to their failure to develop scientific

---

[32] Pierce Butler, *An Introduction to Library Science*, Chicago, University of Chicago Press, 1933, p. XI-XII. (Phoenix Books).
[33] J. Periam Danton, "Plea for a philosophy...," 537.

theories, but instead of calling these a "professional philosophy," he could have added that their pragmatism also led to an equal failure to construct a philosophy of librarianship, so giving the term its true meaning of reflection on the foundations and goals of the discipline.

Librarians and their professors, more concerned with practice than theory, in effect, neglected their more theoretical task, which would have been: research into the philosophical principles of librarianship. Since the pragmatic tendency was a major characteristic of library schools in that era, graduates of these schools could only have taken it with them. The librarian, on leaving the university, conserved this tendency and occupied himself, in the end, with practical work; he had to be more of a technician than a thinker.[34] Uninterested in the scientific principles of the discipline, he was still less interested in its philosophical principles. He lacked an awareness of the importance of reflection on ends and his actions relative to them, and consequently, only rarely concerned himself with the ultimate aims of his institution in society.

Another cause of the weak state of development of library philosophy comes from the fact that librarianship was mainly developed in the United States and Great Britain. In these countries, the dominant school of thought in the 20th century was empiricism, which almost exclusively favored a scientific mode of analysis. In a context of logical positivism, where problems of classical philosophy were considered empty of meaning, one can understand the lack of interest

---

[34] L. Quincy Mumford, "Librarians and the everlasting now," *Library Journal*, 91 (February 15, 1966), 904.

shown by Anglo-Saxon thinkers in a reflection on the ultimate ends of the discipline of librarianship.

The absence of a systematic philosophy of librarianship:

Causes	Consequences
Apprenticeships and gaps in education for the profession	Poorly defined role for librarians
Pragmatic tendency of librarians	Lack of justification in the profession
	Ineffective automated system for bibliographic research
Development of librarianship in Anglo-Saxon countries, steeped in logical positivism, resulting in a disinclination to reflect on the meaning of the practice	Many unresolved problems in the profession

Consequences

The absence of a systematic philosophy of librarianship has engendered a troublesome situation for librarians. Lacking a particularly solid philosophy, librarians find themselves unable to express the principles that form the basis of the existence of the profession. They have a very general idea of their social role and are not capable of responding to the fundamental question: why is their role important?[35]

---

[35] John M. Christ, *Toward a Philosophy...*, 22.

According to Foskett, the lack of a philosophy deprives librarians of the light of reason and of a profound conviction on the value of their work; moreover, it prevents them from developing a sense of continuity.[36]

The absence of a coherent professional philosophy also has the consequence of preventing the development of a truly effective automated system for the diffusion of information.

> The very reason why the engineers have not designed an effective information retrieval device is because we as librarians have not told them what it is we wanted to do, and we have not told them because we do not know. We do not know because we have never developed a philosophy, a theory of librarianship itself."[37]

The lack of interest among librarians in a philosophy of librarianship, considered a secondary activity, has led to a tragic consequence: today, librarians find themselves in a technological world amidst a technological revolution, to which they are having difficulty adapting. They are not ready to live in this world because they have not yet succeeded in precisely determining what role they will play in it. This neglect of fundamental questions has already made it more difficult to find support for libraries. It often means that library advocates rely on the tradition of libraries more than rational argumentation in finding that support.[38]

---

[36] D. J. Foskett, *The Creed of a Librarian...*, 4.
[37] Jesse H. Shera, "What is a book, that a man may know it?" in *Knowing Books and Men: Knowing Computers, Too,* Littleton (Colo.) Libraries Unlimited, 1973, 74.
[38] John M. Christ, *Toward a Philosophy...*, 42

Beyond the problems cited above, the fact of not having a systematic philosophy has also given birth to numerous weaknesses in the profession: a less than rigorous body of theory, weak documentation, a less than shining academic image and a certain confusion concerning the formation of its practitioners. Shera believed that this situation is the source of most of the problems that confront librarians: recruitment, technological development, salaries and work conditions, not to mention the difficulty of improving their image.[39]

Toward a Philosophy of Librarianship

Librarians have a real need for a professional philosophy. They would derive many benefits from it. One of the principal benefits would, without a doubt, be the recognition of the important role they play in society. Actually, libraries receive little attention from sociologists, who ignore their essential functions. For example, Abraham Moles did not mention libraries as an institution with the ability to help individuals avoid being submerged by the fragments of knowledge that are served up by the mass media. Rather, he left the individual to himself, to a personal museum that lets him "create his culture for himself, on a private island."[40]

The library will continue to be deprived of the benefits of sociological analysis until it pronounces its objectives, justify them, and explicitly agrees on the methods it must use to

---

[39] Jesse H. Shera, "Formulate a professional philosophy, in "Diagnosis," *Library Journal*, 88 (January 1, 1963), 50.
[40] Conserve de la communication," in A. Moles and C. Zeltmann, *La communication*, Paris, Denoël, 1971, 143.

attain them.[41] It does not make much difference whether librarianship remains pragmatic or clearly reorients itself as a scientific discipline. Even if it made a thorough application of the scientific method in all of its sectors, librarianship would remain no less a secondary discipline if it does not arrive at a definition of its goals, to justify its existence. It is on this basis that it should receive, not "lip service" as now, but a solid base of support from outside, which would result in stronger library budgets.

Beyond justifying the social function of libraries, the existence of a specific philosophy could only improve librarians' professional status. It would improve their chances of being considered members of an authentic profession that has proved its creativity in developing a set of fundamental concepts for itself. These concepts make the activity of librarians significant in fixing it on well-defined goals. A clear idea of the ends sought defines the methods in use, which makes it easier to achieve those ends.[42]

The development of a systematic philosophy would allow thinkers in library science to evaluate the functions and operations of libraries. "In this way librarianship will be able to meet the challenges of a changing society not only in terms of technical competence but in relevance."[43]

As Shera noted, a well-structured philosophy of librarianship would furnish a base upon which practical aims could be realized and against which the effectiveness of that prac-

---

[41] J. Periam Danton, "Plea for a philosophy...," 543.
[42] A. K. Mukherjee, *Librarianship...*, 30.
[43] John M. Christ, *Toward a Philosophy...*, 25.

tice could be measured.[44] This theoretical base is essential because it assures a structure of continuity that permits the analysis and evaluation of different elements and particular activities of the profession. Furthermore, it allows the possibility for scholars in librarianship to justify their research. They can say that they pursue their studies because libraries aim to achieve such-and-such ends, and that in order to do it, we need such-and-such new knowledge. As it is, no researcher in library science can really claim a justification of this kind.

The development of an authentic philosophy of librarianship would afford librarians a faith and certitude in action that up to now has been missing.[45] A grasp of the ultimate goals would give librarians their "reasons" to do what they do. If they know why they pursue their work, they will do it in a more enthusiastic way. They will have an ideal, a set of convictions and principles to guide and support them in action.

The elaboration of a true philosophy of librarianship would permit librarians to acquire a sense of professional unity. They would be united by their ideals and common goals, and avoid the scattering of the discipline into a multitude of independent specializations.

> The value of philosophy to library science, as to any discipline or body of knowledge, is that it provides a theoretical framework, a structure of continuity within which

---

[44] Jesse H. Shera, "On the importance of theory," in *The Compleat Librarian and Other Essays,* Cleveland, Press of Case Western Reserve University, 1971, 151.
[45] J. Periam Danton, "Plea for a philosophy...," 539.

particular points of view, particular modifications may be analyzed, compared, and evaluated..."[46]

Its Characteristics

According to Raymond Irwin, the philosophy of librarianship should include: a) a definition of librarianship; b) a statement of its goals and objectives; c) a statement of its relationships with other disciplines.[47]

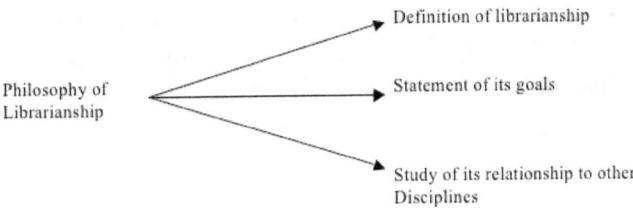

More than identifying, analyzing and interpreting the fundamental concepts from which practice would follow, this philosophy should describe the connection between the profession and the rest of society, because libraries are a social institution, the understanding of which is impossible if left isolated from its social context.

---

[46] John M. Christ, *Toward a Philosophy...*, 17.
[47] Raymond Irwin, *Librarianship: Essays on Applied Bibliography*, London, Grafton, 1949, cited in A. K. Mukherjee, *Librarianship...*, 16.

Myra Kolitsch listed a number of attributes that a real philosophy of librarianship ought to possess.[48] It should, among other things, prove satisfactory to librarians, in the sense that they would possess a proven logic and would be able to justify its forward movement. It should, to be sure, be reconcilable with the social philosophy of the nation to which the librarians who are inspired by it belong. An institution cannot function if it runs contrary to the objectives of the society of which it is an element. Further, it should support rather than hinder the complete development of the individual, of society, and of the library itself. It should be forward-looking, turned toward the future, always self-critical in its adaptation to new realities. Finally, the ideals it proposes should be possible to progressively realize.

---

[48] Myra Kolitsch, "Toward a philosophy of librarianship," *Library Quarterly*, 15 (January 1945), 25.

Part 2

Elements of the Philosophy of Librarianship

Chapter 3
Definition of Librarianship

Despite the absence of a universally accepted philosophy of librarianship, theorists have developed a number of fundamental concepts that allow us to identify some essential elements of a professional philosophy: the nature and goals of librarianship. As pointed out by Raymond Irwin, the first element of a philosophy of librarianship is a definition of it. This is essential because it constitutes the theoretical baseline that provides a way of evaluating the logic and value of advanced ideas in the discipline.[49] Let us find a definition that precisely determines the essential elements of librarianship.

Theorists have already put forth a number of definitions of librarianship. According to Maurice B. Line, "Librarianship should be viewed as a means of communication between knowledge and people."[50] For Danton, "Librarianship or Library Science is that branch of learning which has to do with the recognition, collection, organization, preservation, and utilization of graphic and printed records."[51] Many writers, such as Fussler, think of the library as having a static nature: "The library is to be viewed as a storehouse of men's work of the past and the present or rather of the

---

[49] John M. Christ, *Toward a Philosophy…*, 72.
[50] Maurice B. Line, "Ends and means: librarianship as a social science," *Library World*, 66 (May 1965), 275.
[51] J. Periam Danton, "Plea for a philosophy…," 528.

various records of that work."[52] Others, on the other hand, give the library an essentially dynamic character. For Lucille M. Morsch, for example, "The conception of the library as a center force in a university has developed steadily within the growth of universities."[53]

The preceding definitions cannot be used for our purposes, because they do not give a response to the philosophical question of the nature of librarianship; they aim, rather, to answer the instrumental question: what do libraries do? Their divergence shines a light on the ambiguity that reigns in the profession concerning the discipline's fundamental concepts.

Recently, John M. Christ proposed a new definition:

> Librarianship, or Library Science, is [...] the scientific acquisition, retention, classification, and referral of learning materials required for the preservation and development of knowledge by human subjects in a particular ecological setting.[54]

This definition does not appear usable for our purposes either, in that it lacks universality. It can only be applied to academic and school libraries, due to the focus on learning materials.

---

[52] Herman H. Fussler, ed., *The Function of the Library in the Modern College,* University of Chicago, Graduate Library School, 1954, p. 21.
[53] Lucille M. Morsch, "Acadaemic and research libraries in the United States," in Carl M. White, ed., *Bases of Modern Librarianship,* New York, Macmillan, 1964, 46.
[54] John M. Christ, *Toward a Philosophy...,* 72.

CHAPTER THREE

I am inspired by Jesse Shera's ideas on the aims of librarianship,[55] which suggest the following definition: Librarianship is the art and science of the acquisition, preservation, organization, and retrieval of written and audiovisual records with the aim of assuring a maximum of information access for the human community. The rest of this study will consist of a commentary on this definition and its implications.

Epistemology of librarianship

Our definition affirms the scientific character of librarianship. This affirmation implies an epistemological project, that is to say a reflection on the scientific value of the discipline. To establish its value, it is necessary to undertake a critical study of librarianship, an examination of its foundations: it's aims and its methods. This study on the validity, specificity and unity of librarianship is altogether legitimate, and ought to be undertaken by librarians (library scientists) rather than outsiders, because the epistemology of scientific ideas is more and more the affair of scientists themselves.[56] Specialists in each discipline prefer to assign themselves the task of analyzing the results of their science, rather than leaving the task to philosophers, given that the interest of the latter in the diverse domains of human knowledge does

---

[55] Jesse H. Shera, *Sociological Foundations of Librarianship*, Bombay, Asia Publishing House, 1970, p. 30 (Ranganathan series in Library Science).
[56] Jean Piaget, *Psychologie et épistémologie*, Paris, Editions Gonthier, 1970, p. 11 (Bibliothèque Médiations).

not constitute an end in itself, but rather a way of arriving at a philosophical theory of knowledge in general.

The present study will be limited to establishing the beginnings of an epistemological reflection. A deeper study of the epistemological status of librarianship would necessitate an analysis that is pushed forward by major empirical works within the discipline. I am seeking, rather, to determine if librarianship satisfies the two conditions of being a science: object of study and scientific method. I am attempting to respond to the following two questions: Is there an object of study proper to librarianship? And, is there a scientific method that is applicable to this object?

I do not hesitate to answer both questions in the affirmative. At the same time, it is necessary to state that the scientific aspect of librarianship is rather recent. Traditionally, the work done within libraries was performed in a nontheoretical, intuitive manner. More occupied with practical work than with theoretical development, librarians performed their tasks as determined by local conditions or by tradition. The majority of them have not been particularly concerned with establishing a scientific basis for librarianship, a foundation that would guide practice and institute a separate academic discipline. Besides, most would consider this kind of academic development of little importance. Lawrence Clark Powell illustrates the mentality of the time well when he writes that the desire to serve is the principle quality of a "good" librarian and that a person who possesses such a desire is a true librarian, regardless of whether he has pursued a course of study at a library school or not.[57]

---

[57] Lawrence Clark Powell, "The elements of a good librarian," *Wilson Library Bulletin*, 32 (March 1958), 45.

CHAPTER THREE

The practical orientation of librarians and the weakness of the theoretical base of the discipline could be a sufficient reason to consider librarianship as an art or a technical field rather than as a genuine science. But since its early days librarianship has undergone significant transformations. Noted figures in the profession have quickly pointed out that the doctrines and methods of yesterday's librarians would not be sufficient in the world of today.[58] They have united their efforts in order to leave behind the domain of pure technique and enter the world of science and research. They have spared no effort to provide librarianship, as a discipline, a scientific rigor that it had formerly lacked. The result has been a sudden and profound shift, from pre-scientific to scientific librarianship. Librarians have, in the process, definitively left the realm of routine and improvisation.

Joseph Nitecki demonstrated the scientific character of library studies as much in terms of its object as its method.[59] It is plain that the object of librarianship – the totality of its operations, its techniques, its services, etc., having to do with the world of libraries – is a collection of objective phenomena subject to scientific study. Further, scholars in librarianship make use of methods used by other scientists.[60] They

---

[58] Jesse H. Shera, "Bibliothéconomie, documentation, et sciences de l'information," *Bulletin de l'Unesco à l'intention des bibliothèques*, XIX (mars-avril 1968), 68.
[59] Joseph Z. Nitecki, "Reflection on the nature and limits of library science," *Journal of Library History*, 3 (April 1, 1968) 104.
[60] On the methodology of librarianship, see Herbert Goldhor, *An Introduction to Scientific Research in Librarianship*. Urbana (Ill.),

begin by gathering facts through a method of observation, classifying these facts, proposing a hypothesis to explain them, and, finally, verifying their hypothesis by testing it. F.A. Sharr has given a good summary of the characteristics of the method utilized in library science:

> First, the assembly of data, then its codifications, then the formulation of hypotheses to explain the data, followed by testing of the hypotheses and the derivation of principles, then the extension and amendment of these principles to embrace a wider and wider range of data and thence growing understanding of the total subject area of professional activity.[61]

Contemporary library science has moved beyond intuitive observational knowledge, formed as it is out of concepts that imply the domain described by independent variables that account for observed situations. In short, library science in its present state results from an ongoing conceptual conquest through the invention and putting to work of explanatory models that are ever more exhaustive and coherent with experience. Thanks to the application of the scientific method, librarians suffer less and less confusion between immediate experience and the knowledge base of library science. In becoming scientific, this knowledge base can become intelligible by the judicious application of an adequate conceptualization and a fertile explanatory process.

University of Illinois, Graduate School of Library Science, 1972 (Monograph, no. 12).
[61] F. A. Sharr, "Silent upon a peak in Darien; Presidential Address to the Library Association of Australia 1969," *Australian Library Journal*, 18 (October 1969), 306.

One can conclude, then, that contemporary library science is a science, not by virtue of a decree that says the discipline will be such, but simply because librarians, in applying the scientific method to the domain of librarianship, have produced a systematic collection of ideas that can be qualified as scientific. As libraries are the result of human activity, one must consider librarianship as a social science: "It may be stated categorically that modern librarianship is a social science."[62] Our discipline is an authentic social science in which its object is, to be sure, more circumscribed than other social sciences, because it is limited to a very specific *milieu*: libraries.[63]

Unlike most other social sciences, which are primarily concerned with theory, librarianship has mostly developed its practical side, to the neglect of its theoretical side. It would be to its advantage, in correcting this imbalance, to take inspiration from two other social sciences, social psychology and social work, which have both harmonized their dual elements of theory and practice.[64]

In the definition of librarianship that we have here proposed, we have identified something that is the same time an art and a science. In actuality, it cannot be denied that librarianship today is still far from a total theory of the domain of libraries, that is to say a complete scientific conception of the field. Despite many studies that will be performed in the future, many areas of the daily work of librarianship will never be converted into science. They will continue to be a part of "the art of librarianship," a practi-

---

[62] A. K. Mukherjee, *Librarianship...*, 7.
[63] John M. Christ, *Toward a Philosophy...*, 10.
[64] *Ibid.*, 10.

cal knowledge that guides the work of libraries according to certain rules. In sum, librarianship is a science to the extent that it develops a scientific knowledge base, and also an art, as Broadfield[65] held, at the level of its application.

From Subordination to Autonomy

The more or less scientific orientation that librarianship has taken on obliges librarians to revise many of their long-held positions. One of these concerns the supplementary and secondary character that has been attributed to libraries. The library literature is rich with statements about this. For example, Ronald C. Benge states that the function of the university library is to serve the functions of the university.[66] One well-known librarian from Quebec had the same view of the library as performing a secondary, subordinate role:

> If you consider school, college, university librarianship, you might consider that the role of the librarian is a supplement to that of the teaching staff, as the assistants of both professors and students."[67]

Vleeschauwer expresses this distinction explicitly: "The library is not an autonomous being but serves as an instrument."[68]

---

[65] A. Broadfield, *Philosophy of Librarianship*, London, Grafton, 1949, p. 60.
[66] Ronald C. Benge, *Libraries...*, 226.
[67] Edmond E. Desrochers, "Philosophy of librarianship," *Catholic Library World*, 33 (October 1961), 96.
[68] H. J. Vleeschauwer, "Ambiguities...," 11.

This vision of libraries as secondary institutions with the principle role of "service" has considerably retarded the development of library science, because it has placed theory – the principles and knowledge base of the discipline outside of professional practice – in a region outside the sphere of influence of librarians themselves.[69] If such a conception persists, a science of libraries would become impossible.

> While the library does maintain relationships with elements in the social sphere it must – if it is an independent science – not be dependent on or find direction outside of itself. If the philosophy of library science is not integral to librarianship then librarianship has no philosophy and there is no science; however, this is effectively what is being said in the profession.[70]

We must stop thinking of the library as a secondary endeavor whose goals escape it. We should rather see it as an independent institution that fixes its own specific goals. Even as the library is an independent social institution, it clearly maintains relationships with other institutions, but it nevertheless preserves its autonomy and preserves its ability to determine its aims for itself.

---

[69] John M. Christ, *Toward a Philosophy...*, 48.
[70] *Ibid.*, 47.

Chapter 4
The Ultimate Aims of Libraries

Having discussed the scientific nature of library science, we still have to discuss its humanistic value, that is, its importance to the good of humankind. The vast human project of the Library can only be evaluated according to the aims toward which it is directed. It is because it is founded on the goals it pursues that we are able to judge whether the library does or does not play a fundamental role in contemporary society. The determination of the aims of libraries constitutes the second concern of the philosophy of librarianship. This task amounts to research into the ends that justify the existence of libraries. Why libraries?

History of the Aims of Libraries

To better respond to this question, I will use a historical perspective as a way of becoming familiar with the functions that libraries performed in the past. At the level of ultimate aims, the history of libraries is divided into two distinct periods. The first extends from antiquity through the middle of the nineteenth century. It was characterized essentially by the aspects of "conservation" and "organization." In antiquity, librarians were scholars who worked at the organization and classification of texts. In this way, at the library at Alexandria, librarians preserved ancient culture and assured the control of texts through a method of systematic classification of all recorded knowledge.

In the middle ages, the importance accorded to conservation is yet more evident. Libraries in monasteries were not arranged in the ways we are familiar with, but simply had small rooms with a collection of books. It is thanks to these monks' dedication to the protection of ancient books that they have rendered such an essential service to humanity in saving the thoughts of Roman antiquity. As for university libraries, they are acquainted with the period of the enchained book. Books were laid flat on inclined desks and attached to them with chains. That tidy arrangement sufficiently shows the importance that they accorded to the preservation of books as opposed to their diffusion and sharing. Librarians of the time would insist that "the right book was in the right place on the right shelf."[71]

During the seventeenth and eighteenth centuries, the librarian` played fundamentally the same role as before. He continued to be a scholar who satisfied the needs of intellectual elite who came to study texts on site. Libraries continued to be devoted to the preservation of old books and were used only by a small number of literary people.

The middle of the nineteenth century saw the end of the first phase of the library history. It was in this era that librarians radically revised their attitude in regard to the goals of their institutions. Inspired by the democratic ideals of the Age of Enlightenment, they wanted to make available the wealth of written knowledge that had been the privilege of a few. To the religion of conservation they added distribution. They proposed to communicate knowledge through the utilization of the resources held in libraries. The scholar-librarian, whose principle function had been the conservation of the intellectual treasures of humanity, ceded his place

---

[71] John E. Burke, "Cultural responsibilities of the librarian," *Wilson Library Bulletin*, XXIV (June 1950), 739.

to the active librarian who has faith in the humanity's capacity for self-improvement and considers his institution as a valuable instrument for educating the masses. The library is placed in service to the public, to inform it and to help it become a knowledgeable and rational electorate. From being a simple storehouse, the library became an agent of education that dropped the traditional barriers and allowed free access to the books on its shelves.

Since this radical change, this enthusiasm for a democratization of culture, librarians have not succeeded in creating a unanimous vision of the social role of libraries. Some continue to consider the library essentially a storehouse; some say that it is an educational institution; and others, finally, call it an agency of information diffusion.

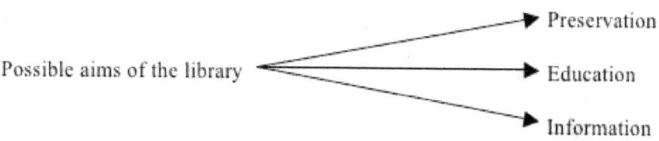

These different conceptions persist today because the fundamental goal of libraries has not yet been definitively established. Let us attempt to shed some light on this essential question within contemporary librarianship.

Libraries and Preservation

Some librarians have maintained a certain nostalgia about the traditional function of the profession, so that they continue to hold that their most important role still consists in guarding and preserving books. For example, according to Gregory, "We, librarians, are the guardians of these written records of [mankind]."[72] F. Allen Briggs also has an anachronistic conception of the role of librarians: "Librarians are bookkeepers or guides – the statement has so often been repeated that library ears ache from its sound; but they are."[73]

There is a grain of truth in the two preceding quotations. They exaggerate a point of view that is nonetheless valid. It is true that librarians must preserve books. It is an essential condition of all else that they do. Without books, without texts, librarians can do nothing, can attain none of their goals. But there is a difference between a necessary function and an ultimate aim. The conservation of texts is not the ultimate aim of librarianship.

The library is much more than a simple storehouse and the librarian much more than a guardian of books. Unfortunately, many librarians have maintained this idea, and a good number express this view, whether aware of it or not, in their actions, their work being limited solely to this function. This attitude can have a most disastrous result for the profession. The great public, including its intellectuals, place the librarian of the first half of the twentieth century together with the book as a physical entity, in his care and protection, more than for his scholarly knowledge of its content. The status of librarians has accordingly lowered. He has still, moreover, not replaced that part of his prestige.

---

[72] Lee H. Gregory, "What makes a good librarian?" *Wilson Library Bulletin,* 34 (September 1959), 47.
[73] F. Allen Briggs, "Librarian: Cerberus or Hebe?" *Wilson Library Bulletin,* 34 (September 1959), 40.

Today, librarians are no longer associated with the intellectual and professional world.

It is evident that if the role of the librarian only consists in preserving texts that he is merely a technician and can not be considered a professional, nor scientific. The function of preservation is not the final goal pursued by librarians.

> It is the intellectual book, not the physical book, that defines the mission of the library and makes it the force that society has the right to expect it to be. It is the librarian as keeper of the intellectual book, and only by necessity of the physical book, that his professional identity is to be sought.[74]

Libraries and Education

Many thinkers give libraries an essentially educational goal. Notably Mukherjee, Broadfield, and Shera. The latter has explained his conception in an article entitled, "Apologia pro Vita Nostra":

> But we insist that the primary responsibility of the library is educational – to stimulate the intellect, to broaden the reader's experience, and challenge him into new avenues of creativity. In a very real sense the library is the laboratory of the mind."[75]

For Mukherjee, "the principle function of the library ... is to serve the cause of education, which brings in its wake a se-

---

[74] Jesse H. Shera, "Apologia pro Vita Nostra," in *Knowing Books and Men...*, 117.
[75] *Ibid.*, 116.

ries of activities by the librarian."⁷⁶ As for Broadfield, the fiercest defender of the educational role of libraries, his vision of the library takes on an almost aristocratic dimension:

> To help in the creation of a community of thinking men, holding opinions independently arrived at, is the main task of librarians. Without libraries, a community of seekers after knowledge would be impossible.⁷⁷

All of these thinkers, whose influence in the world of librarianship has been far from negligible, have considered libraries as an educational institution, one that has as its main function to allow people to educate themselves. Libraries make possible the enriching and instructive reading of the best of humanity's written texts. Over the centuries, this widespread idea has brought about a religion of the book. The love of books and culture has become the principle motivation of the librarian. But it led Shera into a trap, the trap of extreme idealism in maintaining that culture, understood as aiming is wisdom, assures the unity of librarianship.⁷⁸

This is an opportune time to proceed to a demystification of the educational aims of libraries. Libraries, like all other social institutions, are necessarily tied to the historical conditions of their creation, which is to say the initial theoretical and practical methods of their functioning. A naïve librarianship, which forgets the view of its social conditions, ought to be rejected. That is why it is today necessary to set forth the ideas that underlie the practice of librarianship in the

---

⁷⁶ A. K. Mukherjee, *Librarianship...*, 12.
⁷⁷ A. Broadfield, *Philosophy...*, 15.
⁷⁸ Jesse H. Shera, "Isis and the librarian's quest for unity," in *The Compleat Librarian...*, 159.

twentieth century. In maintaining the illusion that the ultimate goal of the library is education, thinkers in library science perpetuate an ideology that is inseparable from the division of society into classes, which exists in the interest of the dominant class. This bourgeois librarianship, which aims to disseminate high culture, to grant access to the treasures of civilization, is alienating for the vast majority of working people.

> And during its early years, when book selection was heavily biased toward reformation and education, it was only the progressive and socially-minded minority who availed themselves of the library's facilities – the general attitude seems to have been one of apathy rather than enthusiasm.[79]

This librarianship is classist also for the reason that it universalizes a system of values that belongs to the dominant class. It is evident that the pursuit of culture and wisdom is not possible for the majority of citizens who, day after day, perform menial and thankless tasks. Moreover, this culture, liberal and contemplative, tends to impose itself as the only possible culture. As Mary Lee Bundy wrote:

> The public library is among the institutions which misuses its public charge to promote one set of cultural values and one cultural heritage as if it were superior to others. Imbedded in this culture and, therefore, in its literary products which libraries carry and promote, are

---

[79] Aileen De Somogyi, "Access versus preservation," *Canadian Library Journal*, 34 (October 1974), 415.

values at complete variance with a democratic society and respect for human worth."[80]

This reproach that Mary Lee Bundy leveled against public libraries can be addressed to other types of libraries, which, even today, aim to spread a unidimensional culture.

Libraries and Information

After having made plain the insufficiencies of the function of preservation and education attributed to libraries as ultimate aims today, it is left to us to examine the more recent tendency, that which considers our institution as being essentially given to the purpose of the distribution of information. From this new viewpoint, the library is an agency of communication that has for its role the communication of messages of importance to members of a community, to give them the ability to be successful in their many activities. Librarians are equivalent to facilitators of communication, who aim to respond to important social needs in transmitting, as quickly as possible, information that is necessary for the life of the community.

This new attitude of librarians seems well justified. In a world that is threatened by an explosion of information, the citizen is flooded by the proliferation of messages, facts and ideas of all sorts. There is a need for an institution – the library – to organize and assemble the various media that contain the information needed to allow him to choose what will be useful to him. The contemporary library becomes a

---

[80] Mary Lee Bundy, "Urban information and public libraries: a design for service," *Library Journal,* 97 (January 15, 1972), 166.

service for information retrieval with the aim of providing all people with pertinent information toward educational, cultural, utilitarian, recreational, or other aims. This new idea returns us to the question regarding readers who would make use of librarians who are animated by a faith in their educational mission. It is not a question of imposing on readers this or that type of information as a pretext for fulfilling a supposed educational or cultural mission. Rather, the librarian leaves it to the user to determine the purpose of his information request and accords him the full freedom to choose for himself the information that he will use. Pierce Butler, who refused to see libraries as an instrument for the education of the masses and entrusted them with the unique responsibility of making use of texts for their own benefit according to their own methods[81], can perhaps be considered as a precursor to this new tendency in contemporary librarianship.

It is by becoming conscious of the specific character of their institutions in providing this informational service that librarians can clear up that ambiguity that reigns in the profession concerning the ultimate aims of libraries, especially school and academic libraries. Many consider these last as pedagogical institutions. In the light of the concept of "information service," it becomes easy to point out the narrowness of that point of view and the danger that it represents for the unity of librarianship. The different types of libraries find themselves with particular aims: support for pedagogy in school and academic libraries, cultural and recreational purposes in public libraries, and the promotion of scientific and technical progress in special libraries.

---

[81] Pierce Butler, *An Introduction...*, 105.

Librarians who work in school and academic libraries who define their institutions in terms of providing pedagogical support defend an idea that is not only contrary to the reality but is dangerous to the existence of the profession itself. To put it succinctly, their philosophy rests on the two following main ideas: school and academic libraries are essentially educational centers, and their librarians are educators who should be perceived as such by administrators, the profession at large, and by the students.

For my part, I do not hesitate to emphasize my opposition to that philosophy, which is largely spread throughout certain sectors. A librarian is not an educator, and he performs particular functions that should not be confused with those of teachers. As Kenneth Kister stated,

> ... [T]he educator is mainly interested in critical analysis of the material involved, whereas the librarian is largely concerned with such services as acquisition, organization, retrieval, and distribution of that material; the first function is essentially substantive in nature, latter procedural. Put yet another way, teaching-learning-scholarship entail making value judgments about subject content, whereas librarianship is (or should be) relatively impartial or neutral toward subject matter.[82]

It is true that reference librarians in academic libraries should, on some occasions, teach students how to use the library in the most effective way. But to use that aspect of the work to justify calling the librarian an educator is not acceptable. Without accusing those who use this argument of bad faith, one can state that they have a poor sense of the

---

[82] Kenneth F. Kister, "A view from the front," *Library Journal,* 96 (October 15, 1971), 3284.

fundamental nature of librarianship. They have neglected to take account of what all types of libraries have as a common goal: the maximal dissemination of information.

Librarians are not engaged in a pedagogical situation, which means they are able to play a role that is completely different from that of a teacher, whose function is normative, hierarchical, and distanced. His fundamental role consists of providing the information requested by the reader, as rapidly and effectively as possible. In academic and school libraries, it is plain that users require, in the majority of cases, information for their educational needs. But it would be an abuse of language to claim this as a reason to call a library an educational institution or a librarian a teacher. The aim here is merely to teach students how to access information.[83]

Librarians who work in school and academic libraries are part of the educational process, not in the role of educators, but as information specialists. Just as one does not call an audio-visual specialist an educator because he supports the pursuit of educational objectives, it is time, I argue, that we recognize the particular role that librarians play in educational institutions.

What reasons could cause so many academic librarians, at colleges and universities, to want at any price to consider themselves as educators? Why do these librarians persist in twisting reality and wearing the mask of teachers? Only the material, concrete conditions in which librarians work can explain their refusal of the simple title of librarian. Recognizing that their status as librarians is relatively low com-

---

[83] Marcel Lajeunesse et al., "La documentation, d'hier à demain," *Documentation et bibliothèques,* 20 (septembre 1974), 134.

pared to professors, and that their salaries are intimately related to their status, these professional non-teachers seek to improve their lot and try to pass as educators. The objective is legitimate. But the path is much less so.

Librarians in school and college libraries should work to improve their conditions not by trying to pass as educators but by recalling and recovering the professional nature of the functions they perform as the information specialists of the organization, in using bibliographic resources for research. It is not in modeling themselves after professors that librarians will succeed in raising their status and their conditions, but rather by showing dynamism in the accomplishment of their essential functions, which no other professionals in school and academic libraries are capable of doing. As information specialists, librarians in all types of libraries should show their solidarity and collaborate in the growth of the scientific knowledge base of the discipline. The future of library science is clearly tied to the construction of a rigorous body of knowledge based on research.

In strongly emphasizing the autonomy of the library in the sphere of education, the appropriate goal of the bibliographic research center, do we not risk turning the library into a service that is folded in on itself, that does not participate in any way in the institutional goals of the classroom? Not at all. I would argue, on the contrary, that the best way for the school or academic library to contribute to the achievement of the educational institution's overall goals consists in pursuing its own aims: maximizing the use of its bibliographic resources. An academic library, scientifically organized, satisfying the information needs of students, professors, non-teaching staff and administrators, and in so doing, adequately fulfilling its unique role in an educational institution, automatically contributes to the realization of the general goals of the educational world.

The contrary thesis, which consists in maintaining that the academic library should marry itself to the general goals of the institution it services, is unacceptable, because it takes away the clarity of the ends of libraries and more or less suppresses the specific nature of the profession of librarianship. If we call the librarian who works in an educational institution an educator, we should, logically, identify librarians who work in special libraries according to whatever projects are pursued by the organizations in which they work, that is, as hospital workers, as paper factory workers, as nuclear engineers, etc. I do not see what common bond can unite librarians who pursue such diverse goals. Furthermore, I do not see what grounds the same professionals could invoke for declaring themselves specialists in the same discipline. Isn't it necessary to acknowledge that librarianship is a unique and distinct entity because it has a specific aim?

Yet, how can we reconcile the autonomy of the library in determining its own aims with the close connections it maintains with the spheres that it serves, particularly the educational sphere? It is clear that the library in an educational institution does not exist independently, for itself. Each is situated in a context in which it must hold itself to account in order to avoid its own isolation and neglect. The general pedagogical goals pursued by an educational institution justify the existence of that institution and determine the nature of its members (professors, students, administrators, etc.), who can explain their presence in terms of their intentions to pursue those objectives, and who need to make use of the library in order achieve them. The goal of an educational institution, then, characterizes the nature of the community that the library serves. The library has an obligation to stay abreast of the information needs of this community in order not to disappear. The attention that is accorded to the scholarly community will have an impact on the different parts of research process and its supporting structures, notably the collection of texts and the choice of indexing terms or level of subject analysis. The educational sphere does not determine the aims of academic libraries, but does exercise a certain influence on many of its processes. The academic or school library pursues the common goals of all libraries: the maximal diffusion of bibliographic resources; in the educational sphere, these resources are selected and dealt with according to the needs of a specific scholarly clientele, which has their own specific information needs.

The academic or school library is definitely not an "educational center," but a bibliographic research system developed in response to the information needs of the educational sphere. The librarian who works in this type of library is not an instructor, but a professional whose proper role consists in executing the functions of this retrieval system that he himself has established: the collection, analysis, organization, and dissemination of information that meets the needs of the educational sphere.

Requests for information can be divided into two types: bibliographic information and factual information. Bibliographic information pertains to bibliographic research meaning, for the user, the identification of texts for use. Factual information consists not in communication regarding texts but in the knowledge that they contain. These two types of information given to users are both legitimate, although bibliographic information has been given a privileged place by librarians since the advent of automated systems for information retrieval, that is, the compilation of bibliographic knowledge through the use of computers.

Much experience with providing factual information, led by American librarians, underlines the importance of this type of information and the necessity of seeing the advantages of a service that has been considered marginal up to now. For example, the celebrated public library of Baltimore, the Enoch Pratt Free Library, has run a "Public Information Center" since 1969.[84] This Center aims only to collect relevant and up-to-date information, without regard to source or how this information might be obtained. Very often, information is collected not through published documents but by direct contact with a range of institutions. This shows the importance that the Center gives to non-published facts or to connections outside of regular channels. The leadership of the Public Information Center have made it a priority to disseminate information in the domain of the health and well-being of the community, having noted that the information needs in this area are at once the most crucial and the least well met.

An information center can also respond to different, but equally vital, needs. For example, to provide information that helps an individual solve problems before they become insoluble or provoke a crisis. Let us allow the director of an information center, or "Contact Centre" as he calls it, describes their service.

> In short, the Contact Centre is just what its name implies. It could be a store front public library branch, or an independent volunteer service by activist librarians,

---

[84] Joseph C. Donohoe, "Planning for a community information center," *Library Journal*, 97 (October 1972), 3284-3289.

or a special place on a college campus. It is information service for survival. It just might be the role model for relevance that we have been trying to build for so long.[85]

An information center can equally interest a user base that is much more deprived: the people who live in ghettos. Mary Lee Bundy[86] emphasizes the urgency of meeting the information needs of disadvantaged citizens. Their information poverty shows the complicity of governments in defending the status quo and their lack of interest in changing the conditions of the poor. The control and manipulation of information is, moreover, one of the many methods in which the inhabitants of ghettos are kept in an oppressive situation. The authorities in place know that they gain and maintain power by restricting access to the information they possess. They are aware that only the well informed can take steps to radically change their situation in society.

Information is a vital issue for people in the inner city. On a daily basis, they deal with serious problems resulting from basic human needs that are not satisfied. Without information that is adapted to their needs, they cannot succeed in changing their life conditions and take control of their destinies.

> Access or lack of access to strategic information can decide the success or failure of individual efforts to solve problems and enhance life opportunities. It is important to the success of efforts to effect even minimal change

---

[85] "The Contact Centre," *Library Journal*, 97 (December 15, 1972), 3959.
[86] Mary Lee Bundy, "Urban information and public libraries: a design for service," *Library Journal*, 97 (January 15, 1972), 161-169.

> and is essential in communities getting and keeping some control over the decisions affecting their welfare.[87]

In providing needed information to all citizens, especially the most disadvantaged, the library lends its support to the realization of democratic ideals: it contributes to the formation of an informed electorate that is capable of rational decisions.

> ... [T]he library is one of democracy's principal agencies for insuring an enlightened citizenry through the promotion of intelligent understanding of economic, governmental, and other social problems.[88]

It should be added that libraries should do much more than share the goal of democracy; they should be democratic in their methods and processes as well. One could say that, in our professional community, this ideal has been attained thanks to librarians' rejection of all forms of censorship: "The library is the most democratic of our institutions. It is a sanctuary of the free mind and an oasis of tolerance."[89]

Librarians working in democratic libraries are professionally neutral in facing political, moral, and religious problems that divide readers. If there is controversy, they defend intellectual freedom, the right of readers to encounter a full range of proposed solutions and answers to their questions, and to choose, in full awareness of their reasons, the ones that seem the most appropriate. For these librarians, what is important is not to impose a certain idea, but to provide this

---

[87] *Ibid.*, 162.
[88] J. Periam Danton, "Plea for a philosophy...," 548.
[89] F. A. Sharr, "Silent on a peak...," 302.

additional opening to the world that allows for informed choices in a state of clarity. They provide free access to all to a collection that contains controversial texts and ideas. This impartiality is made possible by their professional "indifference" to all competing opinions. "If he [the librarian] has no politics, no religion, and no morals, he can have all politics, all religions, and all morals."[90] The contemporary library is a center of liberalism, "but its function is not to preach it but to be liberalism in operation."[91]

---

[90] D. J. Foskett, *The Creed of a Librarian...*, 10.
[91] Joseph S. Dunn, "Functions of a librarian," *Wilson Library Bulletin*, XXVI, (December 1951), 316.

Conclusion

Our approach has led us to find out the ultimate aims of librarianship with a view to why humanity undertakes it as a project. If one posits the distribution of information as its goal, the humanistic aspect of librarianship is established. How can we call a service that aims for the creation of autonomous individuals who are sufficiently well informed to bring about all of their various projects anything but humanistic? This service is all the more humanistic for not forcing its users to sympathize with any aims that might be imposed by an institution. The reader is treated as a true adult who chooses his the information resources he finds useful in pursuing the goals that he has fixed for himself. He has full freedom in making contact with humanity's cultural record to make use of for his own happiness and that of the human community. The work of librarianship is truly a human endeavor, that is to say an activity of humankind for humankind, that has as its end the well being of humankind.

After having established the nature and value of librarianship, at once scientific and humanistic, we can arrive at certain reflections on its limits. The first arises from the irreducible liberty of humankind. Librarians could create the ideal library systems and put in place the best of all possible public programs, but people would still not necessarily make use of them, if they did not make a personal decision to use them to satisfy a need for personal enrichment. The library world only has value in the eyes of the individuals who determine that it has the potential to fill their information needs. The value of libraries only becomes a reality for each human being in that self-determination that has no other name than liberty. There is, at the base of the values of librarianship, an intensively subjective need that can only be answered by undoing the indifference of the individual who faces the world of libraries. "A person who is not self-motivated to gain an education or use information will not do so, no matter how well the education is administered or how efficient the retrieval system."[92]

The limits of literary and scientific production constitute another limit to librarianship. Librarians can only acquire for their readers the works that are actually published. Their action is limited by what is: a finite number of texts, of which they can determine neither the quantity nor the content. If the society that George Orwell described in *1984* should ever become a reality, if civilization should ever reach the point of such inhumanity that it censors publication of works that refuse to propagate the systematic lies of the power structure, libraries would face a choice between a function of indoctrination or disappearance. This threat of the Great Lie reminds us of the severe dependency of libraries. Libraries are a social institution that exists under the pressures of society as a whole. Unfortunately, the study of libraries in their social context, of the influence of political, economic, social and cultural factors on their development has hardly seen a beginning.

Evoking the specter of dictatorship permits us to insist on the profoundly humanistic role of libraries. As an institution of the distribution of information, libraries give each individual the means of critiquing power and, by the same service, prevent the coming of a totalitarian state, which is often

---

[92] Louis Vagianos, "What rough beast a-borning? Educational egalitarianism: lost cause?" *Library Journal,* 98 (June 15, 1973), 1876.

the result of public ignorance. Libraries can be a powerful lever for social transformation. Human progress necessitates a democratization of information that libraries help bring about. How could one imagine the creation of an authentically just society without full and open access to information? Wouldn't a global project of human liberation that does not care about the humanistic aims of libraries risk losing the alienated masses it wants to save? In being a service documentation and research, libraries can surely be considered as "the great potential of society."[93]

---

[93] Verner W. Clapp, "The library, the great potential in our society," *Wilson Library Bulletin,* 35 (December 1969), 307.

Questions for Reflection

1.
Granting Cossette his distinction between library science (study of methods) and library philosophy (study of foundations), have three decades of technological change had implications for library philosophy as they clearly have had for library science? What are those implications, if any? Have the definitions of libraries and librarianship, respectively, been changed along with their contexts and methods? Are its foundations and aims the same as they were at the time of this essay's writing, or something different? If they have changed, what are they now? For example, has the Internet made the informational function of libraries less relevant and made their educational function more attractive?

2.
Cossette noted the lack of agreement about the nature of libraries as a weakness in North American librarianship. He believed that by showing the logical basis of a true philosophy of libraries that everyone could be convinced by it and then, with the same idea in mind, work together toward shared aims more effectively. Can there be agreement about the nature and purpose of libraries, and would it be a good thing if there were? Is the answer to the latter question dependent on the society or the time in which one lives?

3.
Cossette did not find it acceptable for libraries to have a mixture of more than one fundamental goal, that having more than one goal at the same time would result in diffi-

culty in planning or justifying services and make it more difficult to arrive at good decisions and explain what it is that we do. He believed in the power of understanding the essence of a thing. Do you agree with this view? Do you believe that libraries have an essence in the sense that Cossette was looking for?

4.
Do you agree with Cossette's strong assertion that education is a form of indoctrination into bourgeois cultural values and is not as useful as simply providing information? What does education have to offer that Cossette may not have recognized? Do libraries have an educational role? If so, in what way? Who defines the role of libraries?

5.
Cossette talked about the time in which he was writing as a time of rapid change and even technological revolution, as computers were rapidly becoming a part of librarianship. Sometimes the pace of change can make the past appear to lose its relevance, and it is hard to find the time to learn from it anyway. The impressions we have of the past are usually of times when things moved more slowly, but how do we know this? If studying library history surprises us by showing us how things were the same or different in unexpected ways, or shows us how libraries as we think of them came to be what it is, are there potential implications for how we think about what we do? What are those implications?

6.
Contrary to Cossette's assertion that fundamental questions of librarianship received little attention, the list of his cited

works shows that these questions were very much at issue in mid-20th century. Are the same questions at issue today? What is being written on library philosophy now? Are questions of library philosophy being neglected? Are they simply being posed in a "post-library" (or otherwise new) way? Is the library discourse distracted from fundamental questions by more immediate concerns? Can you think of how you might like to "bring library philosophy back," or rephrase the questions currently being asked out there?

7.
Is there a link between the status of librarians in society and the existence (or non-existence) of a philosophy of librarianship?

8.
What are the various ways in which the "science" and "philosophy" in "library science" and "library philosophy" have been and can be understood?

References

Monographs

Benge, Ronald C. *Libraries and Cultural Change.* London, Clive Bingley, 1970.

Broadfield, A. *Philosophy and Librarianship.* London, Grafton, 1949.

Butler, Pierce. *An Introduction to Library Science.* Chicago, University of Chicago Press, c. 1933, 1964 (Phoenix Books).

Christ, John M. *Toward a Philosophy of Educational Librarianship.* Littleton (Colo.), Libraries Unlimited, 1972 (Research studies in librarianship, no. 7).

Foskett, D. J. *The Creed of a Librarian – No Politics, No Religion, No Morals.* London, Library Association, 1962 (Occasional paper, no. 3).

Mukherjee, A. K. *Librarianship, Its History and Philosophy,* London, Asia Publishing House, 1966.

Ranganathan, S. R. *The Five Laws of Library Science,* Madras, 1957.

Shera, Jesse H. *Knowing Books and Men: Knowing Computers Too.* Littleton (Colo.), Libraries Unlimited, 1973.

Articles

Bawa, N. S. "In search of a valid philosophy of librarianship," *Indian Librarian*, 20 (December 1965), 149.

Berthold, A. B. "Science of librarianship," *Wilson Library Bulletin*, 8 (October 1933), 120-121.

Bliss, H. E. "As to a philosophy for librarianship," *Library Quarterly*, 5 (April, 1935), 232-235.

Bontoft, G. J. "Are librarians really necessary?" *Librarian*, 43 (February 1954), 21-24.

Borden, A. K. "We need a philosophy," *Libraries*, 36 (1931), 175-176.

Brewer, J. G. "Geography of librarianship: The Library Association Prize Essay, 1970," *Library Association Record*, 72 (July 1970), 255-257.

Briggs, F. A. "Librarian: Cerberus or Hebe?" *Wilson Library Bulletin*, 34 (September 1959), 39-41.

A. Broadfield, *Philosophy of Librarianship*, London, Grafton, 1949

Broderick, D. M. "I may, I might, I must, some philosophical observations on book selection and practices and the freedom to read," *Library Journal*, 88 (February 1, 1963), 507-510.

REFERENCES

Brown, Margaret C. "A look at the future through bifocals," *Library Resources and Technical Services,* 9 (Summer 1975), 261-269.

Bundy, Mary Lee and Wasserman, Paul. "Professionalism reconsidered," *College and Research Libraries,* 29 (January 1968), 5-26.

Burgess, N. "Librarianship and education," *Library World,* 63 (August 1961), 40-42.

Burke, John E. "Cultural responsibilities of the librarian," *Wilson Library Bulletin,* 24 (June 1950) 739-741.

Burke, Redmond A. "Philosophy of librarianship," *Catholic Library World,* 19 (October 1947), 12-15.

Butler, Pierce. (The cultural function of the library," *Library Quarterly,* 22 (April 1952), 79-91.

_____. "Librarianship as a profession," *Library Quarterly,* 21 (October 1951), 235-247.

Carnovsky, L. et al. "In search of a philosophy," *Library Journal,* 88 (March 15, 1963), 1112-1120.

Chakravarty, N. C. "Librarianship – its philosophy and function," *IASLIC Bulletin,* 4 (March 1959), 10-13.

Chatterjee, A. "Philosophy of librarianship, a literature survey," *Library Herald,* 7 (July-October 1964), 133-137.

Clapp, Verner W. "The library – the great potential in our society?" *Wilson Library Bulletin*, 35 (December 1960), 303, 306-307.

Collison, Robert. "On being a librarian," *Unesco Bulletin for Libraries*, 12 (July 1958), 153-155.

Conant, R. W. "Sociological and institutional changes in American life: their implications for the library," *American Library Association Bulletin*, 61 (May 1967), 528-536.

Cousins, M. "Library in the modern world," *College and Research Libraries*, 20 (November 1959), 454-458.

Cushman, J. "Real business of librarians is education," *Mississippi Library News*, 26 (June 1962), 62.

Danton, J. Periam. "Plea for a philosophy of librarianship," *Library Quarterly*, 4 (October 1934), 527-551.

Desrochers, E. E. "Philosophy of librarianship," *Catholic Library World*, (October 1961), 94-96.

Dollen, C. "And a library is..." *Catholic Library World*, (May 30, 1959), 462-463.

Dunn, Joseph S. "Functions of the librarian," *Wilson Library Bulletin*, 26 (December 1951), 315-318.

Ellsworth, R. W. "Now that we have built," *Louisiana Library Association*, 22 (Summer 1959), 39-41.

REFERENCES

Emery, Richard. "Philosophy, purpose and function in librarianship: the Library Association Prize Essay, 1971," *Library Association Record*, 73 (July 1971), 127-129.

Fairthorne, R. A. "Limits of information retrieval," *Journal of Library History*, 3 (October 1968), 364-369.

Foskett, D. J. "Intellectual and social challenge of the library service," *Library Association Record*, 70 (December 1968), 305-309.

_____. "The library in the age of leisure," *Library Association Record*, 69 (January 1970), 7-10.

Goode, W. J. "The librarian: from occupation to profession," *Library Quarterly*, 31 (October 1961), 306-320.

Gordon, T. Crouther. "The love of books," *Library World*, 54 (March 1953), 147-151.

Gore, Daniel. "Against the dogmatists: a skeptical view of libraries," *American Libraries*, 1 (November 1970), 953-957.

Harwell, Richard. "The magic triad: books, people, and ideas," *Wilson Library Bulletin*, 34 (May 1960), 655-656, 662-663.

Kister, Kenneth F. "A view from the front," *Library Journal*, 96 (October 1971), 3283-3286.

Kolitsch, Myra. "Toward a philosophy of librarianship," *Library Quarterly,* 15 (January 1945), 25-31.

Lethève, Jacques. "Aperçu sur la situation du bibliothécaire scientifique," *Libri* 10 (1960), 46-48.

Line, Maurice B. "Ends and means: librarianship as a social science," *Library World,* (May 1965), 270-275.

McColvin, L. R. "Faith of a librarian," *Indian Librarian,* 4 (June 1949), 1-16.

McCrum, B. P. "Idols of librarianship," *Wilson Library Bulletin,* 21 (September 1946), 41-47.

McMullen, Haynes. "Research in backgrounds in librarianship," *Library Trends,* 6 (October 1957), 110-119.

Marco, G. A. "Old wine in new bottles: the philosophy of librarianship," *Ohio Library Bulletin,* 36 (October 1966), 8-14.

Martin, J. M. "Time Library Association Prize Essay: Librarianship one world," *Library Association Record,* 62 (October 1960), 316-319.

Miller, R. A. "Search for fundamentals, *Library Journal,* 61 (April 15, 1936), 298.

Molz, K. "Education for sensibility in the house of facts," *American Libraries,* 1 (January 1970), 29-32.

Mumford, L. Quincy. "Librarians and the everlasting now," *Library Journal,* 91 (February 15, 1966), 901-906.

Nitecki, Joseph Z. "Public interest and the theory of librarianship," *College and Research Libraries,* 25 (July 1964), 269-278, 325.

_____. "Reflection on the nature and limits of library science," *Journal of Library History,* 3 (April 1968), 103-119.

Ramakrishna, Rao K. "Philosophy of librarianship," *Indian Librarian,* 16 (September 1961), 69-72.

Ranganathan, S. R. "The five laws of library science," *Giranthalaya,* 2 (October-December 1956), 6-13.

_____. "Library science and scientific method," *Annals of Library Sciences,* 4 (March 1957), 19-32.

_____. "Library system and increasing purpose," *Libri,* 7 (1957), 121-144.

Reddy, K. Siva. "The need for philosophy of librarianship," *Indian Librarian,* 25 (September 1970), 81-84.

Rothstein, Samuel. "In search of ourselves," *Library Journal,* 93 (January 15, 1968), 156-157.

Savage, Ernest A. "The faith of a librarian," *Library Association Record,* 62 (March 1960), 79-83.

———. "Man's library: potential and actual; an essay in library philosophy," *Library World,* 49 (December 1946), 56-62, 77-80.

Sharr, F. A. "The proper study of librarianship," *Library Journal,* 96 (November 15, 1971), 3727-3730.

———. "Silent upon a peak in Darien: Presidential address to the Library Association of Australia, 1969," *Australian Library Journal,* 18 (October 1969), 303-315.

Shaw, Ralph R. "The library's role in society today," *Journal of Education for Librarianship,* 2 (1962), 177-182.

———. "Quo vadis?" *Library Journal,* 92 (September 1, 1967), 2881-2884.

Shera, Jesse H. "Bibliothéconomie, documentation et science de l'information," *Bulletin de l'Unesco à l'intention des bibliothèques,* 19 (mars-avril 1968), 62-70.

———. "Formulate a professional philosophy," in "Diagnosis," *Library Journal,* 188 (January 1, 1963), 50.

Shores, Louis. "Philosophy of librarianship," *Library and Information Science* (Japan), no. 9 (1971), 39-48.

Temple, P. L. "Library responsibility," *Catholic Library World,* 21 (November 1949), 35-38.

Vagianos, Louis. "Conversations with a computer," *Library Journal,* 98 (December 15, 1973), 3608-3611.

REFERENCES

_____. "What rough beast a-borning? Educational egalitarianism: lost cause." *Library Journal*, 98 (June 15, 1973), 1873-1879.

Vleeschauwer, H. J. de. "Ambiguities in the present-day library," *Mousaion*, no. 36 (1960), 60p.

_____. "Library science as a science," *Mousaion*, nos. 37-40 (1960), 293p.

Wellard, J. H. "Philosophical approach to library science," *Wilson Library Bulletin*, 9 (December 1934), 206-207.

Index

academic and school libraries, 32, 49-54
access to information, 33, 43, 46-47, 57
 restricting, 55-56, 59
 see also information dissemination
aims, *see* librarianship, aims and goals of
apprenticeship, 18-19
autonomy, 37-39, 52-53
 see also librarians as functionaries and subordinates

Benge, Ronald C., 13, 16, 38
Briggs, F. Allen, 44
Broadfield, A., 18, 37, 45-46
Bundy, Mary Lee, 47, 55
Butler, Pierce, 19-20, 49

causes for lack of philosophy of librarianship, 18-22
censorship, *see* access to information, restricting
Chatterjee, Amitahba, 10-11
Christ, John M., 16, 32-33
Columbia University, 19
consequences of lack of philosophy of librarianship, 2, 22-24, 59-60
continuity, logical, 22-23, 25-26

Danton, J. Periam, 1, 17, 20, 32, 56
democratization, 42-43, 56-57
De Somogyi, Aileen 47

Dewey, Melville, 19
Dunn, Joseph S., 57
Duverger, Maurice, 12

education (field of study), *see* pedagogical science
educational role of librarians, 43, 45-54
Emery, Richard, 13-14
empiricism, 1, 8, 21, 34
ends, *see* librarianship, aims and goals of
Enoch Pratt Free Library Public Information Center (Baltimore), 54-55
epistemology, 33-37

Five Laws of Library Science, The
 see Ranganathan, S. R.
Foskett, D.J., 1, 11, 22-23, 57
Fussler, Herman H., 31-32

Goldhor, Herbert, 7, 35n60
Gregory, Lee H., 43-44

historical perspectives on librarianship, 1-2, 41-43, 46
humanistic role of librarianship, 2-3, 9, 41-42, 58-60
 see also librarianship, aims and goals

impartiality, 50, 57
information dissimation, 48-57
Irwin, Raymond, 26-27, 31

justification for libraries, 1, 5, 24-27
  see also consequences of lack of philosophy of librarianship

Kister, Kenneth, 50
Kolitsch, Myra, 27

L'Ecole nationale superior de bibliothécaires, 18
librarianship, definition of, 31-37
librarianship, aims and goals of, 1-2, 5, 7, 12, 16, 21, 25-27, 33, 41-57
librarianship as science, 1, 8, 20, 34-36-37
  see also scientific method
librarianship as subordinate occupation (secondary, supplemental, merely functionary), 13-14, 37-39
  see also autonomy
  see also technical vs. theoretical occupational practices
Line, Maurice B., 31
logical continuity, *see* continuity, logical
logical positivism, 21

McMullen, Haynes, 11
methodology of librarianship, 35
  see also scientific method
Moles, Abraham, 24
Morsch, Lucille M., 32
Mukherjee, A. K., 11, 37, 45-46

neutrality, *see* impartiality
Nitecki, Joseph, 35

pedagogical science, 15, 53
  see also educational role of librarians
philosophy vs. science, 6-10, 12
Piaget, Jean, 33
Powell, Lawrence Clark, 34
pragmatism, 1, 17, 20
  see also technical vs. theoretical practices
preservation, 41-45, 48
public libraries, 47, 49, 54-55
purpose of libraries, *see* librarianship, aims and goals of

Ranganathan, S. R., 10-13

school libraries, *see* academic and school libraries
schools of library science, 18-19, 21
science vs. philosophy, *see* philosophy vs. science
scientific method, 1, 7, 11-12, 34
Sharr, F. A., 36, 57
Shera, Jesse, 1, 18, 23, 24-25, 33, 45-46
social science, 11-12, 36-37
special libraries, 49, 52

technical vs. theoretical practices, 1-2, 14-15, 19-21, 34-35

unity (of librarianship), 2, 5-6, 8, 26, 49
University of Chicago, Graduate Library School of, 1
University of London (library school), 18

values of librarians, 2, 8, 47, 58-59
Vleeshauwer, H. J., 10, 38

Williamson, C. C., 19

Other Books of Interest from Library Juice Press

Library Juice Concentrate, edited and mostly written by Rory Litwin. ISBN 978-0-9778617-3-6

Library Daylight: Tracings of Modern Librarianship, 1874-1922, edited by Rory Litwin. ISBN 978-0-9778617-4-0

Speaking of Information: The Library Juice Quotation Book, compiled by Rory Litwin and edited by Martin Wallace. ISBN 978-0-9802004-1-6

Barbarians at the Gates of the Public Library: How Postmodern Consumer Capitalism Threatens Democracy, Civil Education and the Public Good, by Ed D'Angelo. ISBN978-0-9778617-1-2

Responsible Librarianship: Library Policies for Unreliable Systems, by David Bade. ISBN 978-0-9778617-6-7

Questioning Library Neutrality: Essays from Progressive Librarian, edited by Alison Lewis. ISBN 978-0-9778617-7-4

From Polders to Postmodernism: A Concise History of Archival Theory, by John Ridener. ISBN 978-0-9802004-5-4

Slow Reading, by John Miedema. ISBN 978-0-9802004-4-7

Information and Liberation: Writings on the Politics of Information and Librarianship, by Shiraz Durrani. ISBN 978-0-9802004-0-9

www.ingramcontent.com/pod-product-compliance
Lightning Source LLC
Chambersburg PA
CBHW052053220426
43663CB00012B/2550